Just What Is...
Network Marketing?

Other Network Marketing books by David Barber

The S.T.A.R. Leadership Programme:

Get Off To A Winning Start In Network Marketing (Feb 1996)
Breakthrough Sponsoring & Retailing (Feb 1996)
How To Lead A Winning Group (April 1996)
Network Marketeers—Supercharge Yourself! (April 1996)

Other Publications:

The Daily Express Guide To Network Marketing

Just What Is...
Network Marketing?

Second Edition

by

David Barber

Fellow of the Institute of Sales & Marketing Management
Fellow of the Institute of Directors

Insight Network Marketing Library

Just What Is... Network Marketing?
David Barber

Insight Publishing Ltd
Serendipity House
Greytree Road
Ross-on-Wye
Herefordshire HR9 7DQ
Phone: 01989-564496
Fax: 01989-565596

Published in association with Cedar Publishing Limited

First published by Cedar Publishing Limited 1993
This revised edition published by Insight Publishing Limited 1996

ISBN: 1-899298-00-2

Cover design by Just Proportion, Louth, Lincolnshire
Printed in Great Britain by Clays Ltd, St Ives plc

Contents

Preface

1 Just What Is This Amazing Way
Of Doing Business? 11

2 What Does It Take To Succeed? 19

3 Common Concerns Covered 23

4 Who Gets Involved? 29

5 What Does It Cost To Get Started? 33

6 What's In It For You? 35

7 How Do You Assess A Company
And Its Product? 41

8 What Can You Offer To People You Know? 47

9 So, What Do You Do Next? 51

Appendix: Corruptions Of The Concept 53

Preface

For many people, network marketing can offer the best—perhaps the only—realistic way to solve a wide range of personal or financial problems, or to realise their ambitions. It is a remarkable business concept which has proved to be successful in helping people from many different backgrounds, from those needing just a few pounds a week from a part-time occupation, to those looking for a major business with almost no investment—or anything in-between.

For these reasons, it is a tragedy to see someone make a decision about whether they should get involved based on a misunderstanding, a poor presentation of the concept or uninformed media coverage. For the concept is as yet little understood and is frequently misrepresented.

My purpose is to show you the marvellous opportunity open to anyone as an **Independent Distributor** within the network marketing industry.

Independent Distributors are completely self-employed, running their own businesses with the minimum of restrictions and the maximum of freedom, with almost no money tied up, with no warehousing, staff or premises and with almost no stockholding—yet capable, if they so wish, of earning exceptional incomes from high-level businesses.

Network marketing is a great way of doing business, but ***this does not necessarily mean that it is right for YOU***! In fact, if you:

• Enjoy your present occupation, with a good boss or good staff, good prospects, good security...

• Are totally happy with your income...

• Have enough time to appreciate the people who matter to you and the things which interest you (family, friends, pastimes, holidays)...

...Then network marketing may not be right for you at this stage. You have a pretty good life at the moment, so why risk upsetting the balance?

But, although you may be happy with life now, what would happen if you were to lose your occupation or your business, or have an unexpected change of boss in, say, three months time? Might not network marketing then become the answer to your problems? Therefore, it may still repay you to take a close look at the concept.

Most people, especially in today's harsh economic climate, have few options if they lose their occupation or business. You, however, now have the security of knowing that you do have an attractive alternative should such misfortunes come your way.

It may sound flippant to say that a hammer-blow like redundancy to a 50 year-old or the shattering of a dream through bankruptcy is a blessing in disguise, but many people have said to me that having 'discovered' network marketing, in hindsight, redundancy was the best thing that had ever happened to them—and one wonders if a bankrupt would have put so much effort behind succeeding had they *not* been financially embarrassed when they came in?

Whether it is 'yes' or 'no', the decision you have to make is an important one—for both you and your sponsor[1]. If a decision to come into the business turns our to be wrong, your sponsor will have wasted a lot of valuable time and effort in helping you to get your business off the ground; and you will have wasted time which would have been better spent elsewhere.

But, if the opposite happens and you do not come in when in fact you should have done, not only will your sponsor have lost a potentially good Independent Distributor for their business, but you will have lost even more by missing out on possibly the biggest opportunity to come your way.

For it to be the right decision for **both** *of you, it has to be the right decision for* **you**. And, to make the right decision for yourself, you need to make sure that your investigations are *open-minded*.

All businesses, all professions, have their disreputable elements and network marketing is no exception[2]. Our unprofessional elements are just as much hated by true network marketeers as rogue doctors or builders are abhorred by their more professional colleagues.

So it is no more sensible to judge this business by its abusers than it is to judge the medical profession or the building business by their rogues.

So the purpose of this booklet is to:

• Discover what network marketing actually is

---

[1] If you become an Independent Distributor, your sponsor will be the person who introduces you to this business. It may well be that you have been lent this book by a potential sponsor.

[2] For corruptions of the system, see the Appendix on page 53.

- Uncover some popular misconceptions; in other words, what it is *not*

- See if we can help you to decide whether or not network marketing is something you should get involved in

- If you do decide to get involved, help you to choose a reputable company.

As in any business, companies vary in the way in which they apply the concept and in their reward structure; so you should get this information direct from any company you may be interested in or, if you were lent this booklet by an Independent Distributor, from him or her.

~ ~ ~

For further information about the UK industry, contact:

The Direct Selling Association (DSA),
29 Floral Street, London
WC2E 9DP
(phone 0171-497 1234).

The Association works closely with the Department of Trade and Industry, the Office of Fair Trading and various other bodies, as well as the leading network marketing companies, to preserve the integrity of the industry.

The Department of Trade and Industry has issued a useful booklet on the network marketing industry and this is available from the DSA.

For international addresses, see page 56.

Chapter 1

Just What Is This Amazing Way Of Doing Business?

I have in my time been a trainee lawyer, personnel officer, director of a dozen companies, entrepreneur earning in excess of six figures, and writer of eleven books. I have also been a sought-after consultant and trainer and been appointed to numerous professional bodies. I am one of those truly lucky people who can pretty much choose how to make their living.

So, when someone first approached me about network marketing I rejected it out-of-hand for all those familiar reasons: it is a scam, pyramid selling, unethical, immoral, not a proper business to be involved in, should be made illegal ... I am sure you have heard all these criticisms and more. But what makes me even more ashamed than my arrogance in dismissing something about which I thought I knew a lot but in fact knew nothing, was that I did not treat the poor distributor with the respect I now realise his profession thoroughly deserved!

It took a complete accident to change my attitude and make me realise what an ignoramus I had been. Directly against my advice, someone who means a great deal to me insisted on going to what I now know is called a Business Opportunity Meeting, so *I* insisted on going along to protect her interests and make sure she was not 'conned'! To my amazement I found that the people at the meeting were not the 'wide boys' I had expected but a complete cross-section of society, including serious businesspeople and professionals. It took me a while, because my previous business and sales preconceptions kept getting in the way, but I have come to realise that for the *right* person and for the *right* product there is no better way of getting the product from the supplier to the customer. But, much more important than that for me, I grew to understand that *no* other way of doing business has so many socially desirable aspects than *properly run* network marketing.

So, as I said in the chapter heading, just what is this amazing way of doing business? Network marketing is one of the 'chains of distribution'. The chains of distribution are the different ways in which a supplier or manufacturer can get their product from their premises or factory gate to the end-consumer (you or me buying it for our own use).

What are the main chains of distribution?

1. **Traditional Retailing**. This is where the product goes from the supplier $\Rightarrow$ perhaps through one or more distributors $\Rightarrow$ to a wholesaler $\Rightarrow$ to a retailer $\Rightarrow$ and then you or I buy that product from the retailer.

2. **Mail Order or Direct Mail**, where the customer orders direct from the company in response either to advertising in the press or on TV, or to the never-ending barrage of leaflets and mail coming through your letter box, with which we are all so familiar!

3. **Direct Selling**. Which is selling to end-consumers in their homes or at their places of work. There are three main ways of doing this:

- Direct salespeople (often via catalogue drops)
- Party Plan
- Network marketing

You can see from this that network marketing is considered to be a branch of direct selling. *However, direct salespeople and network marketeers are very different people.* The way they work is quite different and the way a company deploys a direct salesforce should also be quite different from the way it deploys a network of Independent Distributors.

The proof that this is not a traditional sales business is that probably 95% of people who become network marketeers neither are, *nor will want to be*, trained salespeople in the traditional sense.

In fact, network marketing does not need trained salespeople nor, indeed, any form of previous business experience because it is based on three remarkably simple ideas:

1. *Get a product you can be proud of and show it* to people you know—friends, relations, neighbours and acquaintances or to people introduced to you by them

2. With the help of people already experienced in the business, *show a simple business opportunity* to friends, relations, neighbours and acquaintances or to people introduced to you by them

3. In your own time, and as your confidence, knowledge and experience grow, *in a very simple way, teach people coming into your business to do the same.*

How does network marketing differ from traditional business?

Traditional companies who use salespeople or distributors, give them a strictly defined local area; but a company using network marketing as its chain of distribution gives you and me the right to handle its products by setting up our own businesses in all the national and international markets in which the company is operating.

We then expand our businesses by introducing or 'sponsoring' other people to do the same. They in turn expand their businesses by sponsoring others to do the same, and so on down the levels.

The big advantage of the sponsoring system is that, by introducing just a few people yourself and everyone else doing the same thing, you can relatively quickly finish up with a large network of Independent Distributors.

How does this work?

Let's say, for example, that you sponsor only *five* people yourself and everyone you bring in just happens to follow suit, then you would have a business which is growing as in the following chart:

• On Level 1 is just yourself[1]

---

[1] Some companies say that you are your own Level 1: others define your level 1 as the people you sponsor. For the purposes of this example, the difference is not important.

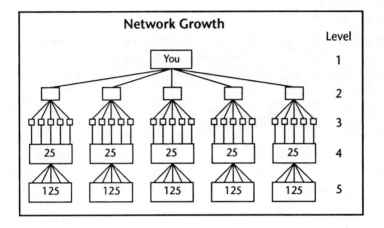

- Level 2 has 5 people on it—the people *you* have sponsored
- The 5 people you sponsored, each bring in 5 Independent Distributors and this gives you 25 people on Level 3
- The 25 Independent Distributors on Level 3 each bring in 5 people and this gives you 125 people on Level 4
- The 125 Independent Distributors on Level 4 each bring in 5 people and that gives you 625 people on Level 5.

Add all the levels together and, although *you* brought in only 5 people (and no-one else has done more), you now have 781 people (including yourself) in your business.

Another major difference between network marketing and traditional retailing is in the much simplified distribution system used by network marketing. Believe it or not, in the traditional retailing system, between 60% and 90% of the retail price of a product (excluding taxes, of course) is soaked up by distributors, wholesalers and retailers. *Each time* the product passes through another set of hands, these outlays get added to the basic cost: rent, rates, services, wages, cost of stockholding, write-offs for damaged or non-selling stock, pilferage, financing of cashflow, insurance, and profit for *every* distributor, wholesaler and retailer in the chain. There may also be costs added on by each pair of hands for salesforces, advertising and sales promotion.

In network marketing, the Independent Distributor replaces all of these functions. In some network marketing companies, goods may be delivered to the customer directly from the supplier, but the Independent Distributors will still receive their commissions in return for finding the customer and taking the order.

You can now see why it is that network marketeers can earn such high incomes. This clearly shows that high incomes are *not* the result of a network marketing company inflating the price of the product, as has been claimed; they come instead from the company 'saving' the costs incurred in the traditional retailing system, and re-distributing these very substantial savings to their Independent Distributors[2].

How big is network marketing?

Network marketing (then known as MLM, or Multi-level Marketing) was established in the early 1940s.

Since then, it has become a fast-expanding part of the American business scene. By 1990, the industry was

---

[2] That is not to say that some companies do not try to move over-priced product through network marketing. But if they do they are destined to fail. It is easy enough to find out if a product is over-priced, and I would suggest that you avoid such companies.

moving some $15 billion worth of goods, and it is still expanding rapidly.

Its success has been such that *The Wall Street Journal* forecast that it would be one of the most powerful influences on the market-place in the '90's. *Fortune Magazine* agreed, calling it '...the most powerful way to reach consumers in the '90s'.

Turning to the British scene, Peter Clothier, a top selling British writer on network marketing, described it as 'The business opportunity of the 1990s'. His credentials for making such a strong statement?—Peter was a Trading Standards Officer and spent his last seven years there leading a Special Investigations Unit. Could there be a better place from which to see just how genuine any business concept actually is?

Although the concept is considered a new one in the UK, the level of business being done here is surprising: by 1992 *The Observer* estimated that 500,000 people—a population the size of Liverpool—were already involved, largely on a part-time basis. That represents about 1.5% of the working population. Yet the concept has hardly begun to take root over here!

So what are the prospects for the industry?

The benefits of properly-run schemes for everyone concerned—manufacturers, distributors and consumers— are so compelling that it is difficult to envisage anything other than an explosion of growth in the UK over the next few years, Anyone joining now is in at the beginning of a revolution and countless people will live to regret having said 'no' without a proper look at the concept.

The concept is already well-proven. The question for any aware person is no longer, 'How does network marketing stack up against my present method of earning a living?' but rather, 'How does my present method of earning a living stack up against network marketing?'

All that remains is for you to decide whether you want to be part of it.

Chapter 2

What Does It Take To Succeed?

It might surprise you to learn that network marketing is so simple that no previous sales, management or business experience are needed to succeed.

Nor do you need any particular talents, educational standards, background, advantages, or skills. This is because the skills and attitudes you need to succeed are so simple that anyone can acquire them.

You do not even have to be particularly good at the skills that *are* needed, (many of the *top* distributors are not!) because you can compensate simply by doing more. It is not how good *you* are which is the issue, it is how good your people are. Sooner or later, the right number of people with the right level of competence will appear—they always do—*provided you keep working at it.*

Although I have said that the business is simple, this is not the same thing as saying it is easy. To explain what I mean, the technique of walking is something which most of us find simple, but few of us would say that walking twenty miles is easy! In the same way, the determination that most people need to succeed in network marketing is also not easy.

So just what is required?

This depends on what you want out of the business. If you are looking only for a small extra monthly income, this may be satisfied by 'retailing', selling or 'showing' the product to enough people to ensure that you get that monthly income.

Over a certain income requirement, you will need to build a small or large group of Independent Distributors. If this is your aim, success will mean developing the right Attitude:

- Have pride
- Have confidence
- Be unstoppable
- Be teachable
- Have patience

If we have a brief look at each of these:

1. **Have pride.** This means having pride in:

- The Company
- The Product
- Network Marketing
- Yourself in taking action to improve your future.

Pride in what you are doing is of course essential if you are going to introduce the product and the business successfully to other people. Pride will also give you the strength to deal with any problems you may experience later, and the motivation to want to be successful.

2. **Have confidence.** Pride in your product, your company and network marketing will help to give you the confidence you need to develop your business. But you also need the confidence in yourself that you can do it.

3. **Be unstoppable.** This means: whatever obstacles you meet, just keep on going and never stop!

4. Be teachable. Although this is a simple business, it is a very different way of doing business and it can be unforgiving of Independent Distributors who do not stick to a proven, simple but narrow path.

But there is no point in being teachable if the training you get is inadequate. With most companies, training is in the hands of the Independent Distributors themselves and therefore the quality can vary tremendously even within the same company.

So, if you are going to be serious about your success in the business, I would strongly suggest that you make your sponsor commit to giving you the support you will need before you sign up with him or her.

5. Have patience. Of course, any business takes time to build and, in this respect, network marketing is no different. The difference here, though, is that those people who do exercise the patience required to build a solid business can look forward to an income possibly far in excess of any they could have hoped to earn by any other means.

To be successful, you must, of course, also make sure that you get involved with the right company and the right product. This is the subject of Chapter 7.

Chapter 3

Common Concerns Covered

If Independent Distributors have no set areas, doesn't this result in people from different groups falling over each other in their local area?

It certainly sounds as if this would happen but, in practice, this is not a problem because Distributors recruit from people they know and they tend to have different contacts even when they are living close to each other. Far from local Independent Distributors seeing each other as competitors (which is precisely what would happen in traditional business if you were to have agents without clearly defined local areas), local network marketeers, in every network I have ever seen, do the complete opposite and band together to help each other.

This is one of the great attractions and it can surprise people from a corporate background, who are used to the in-fighting and company politics so typical of that arena. A spontaneous willingness to help each other is a hallmark of true network marketeers.

Surely, looking at the network marketing growth chart on page 15, schemes must saturate fast!

On the figures we worked on, yes, it would look as if you could have the whole population of the UK in your business after only six months! Again, this simply does not happen in practice as, sadly, only a proportion of new distributors will be motivated to do much with the opportunity.

Founded in 1959, Amway is the biggest network marketing company in both the world and in the UK. Herbalife, another major international network marketing company, has been in the UK since 1983. Yet do *you* know an Independent Distributor from *either* company—let alone both? If you do, I can assure you that you are in the minority.

To prove this point, I ask at my training sessions whether anyone present actually knows an Amway or Herbalife Distributor. Very rarely do more than one or two people in ten put their hands up. Both companies, despite having been in existence for so long, complain that they cannot get enough Distributors.

People keep talking about sponsoring but no-one seems to mention selling. Surely, someone has to sell something?

The network marketing growth chart on page 15 showed an example business of 780 Distributors. If all of your 780 people were part-time and averaging only *one sale a week each* worth, let's say, only £50 per sale, this could (depending on your company) *earn you £5,000 a month!* Only *two* sales a month each *would still earn you £30,000 a year!* Network marketing is a lot of people doing a little bit, not, as in conventional business, a few superstars doing a lot.

Surely I must need sales skills!

This is a common misconception and understandably so because, looked at from the outside, it does look as if salespeople must have a real advantage. In fact, as will become clearer in the next chapter, there is not a lot in common between a traditionally trained salesperson and a network marketeer. In other words, you do not need conventional sales skills to succeed.

However, you will need to be able to get on with the three groups of people who will form the basis of your success: potential distributors, distributors already in your business and customers of the product.

No doubt you are used right now to discussing things with people, telling people things, showing people things and recommending things to people. The skills you will need to show the business, show the product and teach your Distributors to do the same are only a slight refinement of these activities, activities which you already do on a daily basis.

Even if I don't need sales skills, surely it would help if I came from a business background?

This, too, is not borne out by experience. Businesspeople, in fact, are the worst sceptics where network marketing is concerned. Why? Because:

- After years of working in conventional business, they often cannot believe that any business so simple can actually work!
- Network marketing overturns so many of the accepted conventions of other types of business that this can make it difficult for them to understand
- Over the years, there has been a certain amount of unfavourable publicity, some of it caused by corruptions of the concept and some caused by uninformed media coverage. Businesspeople are more likely to be aware of this and are therefore more likely to be affected by it.

In fact, remarkably few business skills are required because your company takes all the more complicated and technical aspects of running the business off your hands. The main skill you will need is your ability to get on with people, as we discussed above, very much as you get on with people now on a daily basis, but with simple refinements.

The main requirements, as we discussed earlier, are definitely ones of **Attitude,** in which matters like skills, experience and background have no relevance. In fact, based on the American experience, the most successful single group are women teachers. No sales or business skills there!

As you saw, I found to my own cost that the preconceptions sometimes held by businesspeople and salespeople can make it difficult for them to accept that network marketing is different and that there is a new skill to be learnt. This is a pity because those who do embrace a different way of doing things are then in a position to turn their previous skills to advantage. But I am afraid that it is more common to see them being overtaken by people who come to the concept without business experience but with an open mind and a willingness to learn.

Isn't this Pyramid Selling?

Pyramid Selling is the opposite side of the coin to network marketing, just as a 'cowboy' builder is the opposite side of the coin to a professional builder. It is easy to spot the difference (probably easier than spotting a 'cowboy' builder!) and this is fully covered in the Appendix on page 53.

I don't want to put my friends through the embarrassment of saying 'No' to me

Quite honestly, I am embarrassed at the thought of selling to people I know

I don't want to lose my friends

This means having to sell, and I don't think I would be good at it

These are all different ways of expressing the same fear or concern—that of approaching people one knows. But there is no need to worry because no-one is expecting you to go 'door-knocking' or twisting people's arms. Nor will you be asked to pin your friends and neighbours to the wall until they buy!

It has to be said that many distributors do try high-pressure techniques and stories are legion of neighbours rushing indoors or hiding behind the garden shed as their local network marketing distributor approaches. Or of people turning up for a dinner invitation, only to find that a blackboard appears from behind the curtains with the coffee and they are subjected to a sales-pitch!

What people don't tell you is that these distributors *never* succeed! This is precisely how *not* to do it.

The aim of network marketing is to have more friends, not fewer! If you apply pressure or are aggressive, yes, you will embarrass or lose your friends. But you will also lose in another way: *an important part of this business is to ask people you know to recommend you to people they know.* Would they do this if they felt pressured by you or unhappy at the way you had dealt with them?

Approaching people you know and keeping their friendship is governed by the understanding:

> *It is not the asking which offends your friends, it is the pressure. No-one minds being asked.*

In fact, if you have a product and an opportunity you are proud of and ask in the right way, most people will be pleased at your interest, even if they say 'No' to what you are offering.

Because we in the industry want to avoid traditional 'selling' at all costs, we never use that word. Instead, we use words like, 'showing', 'sharing', 'inviting' or 'asking' and, where the product is concerned, 'retailing' to describe what we do. This means that you show your friends and contacts a realistic picture of what the business and the product are all about and then let them make up *their own* minds without pressure from you.

This a business where the word will soon get around about you: either that you are a pleasure to deal with, or that you are *not* a pleasure to deal with. If you sell someone a product that is unsuitable for them, the word will soon spread. On the other hand, satisfied customers will happily refer you to their friends and spread a good word about you.

The easiest people to sell to should be existing customers—but only if they feel comfortable with you! So there is no conflict between the way you relate to people in your business and personal life: honesty, integrity and consideration for their feelings will always pay in the long run.

Yes, you will want to show the opportunity or the product to as many people as you can, but you will do it with consideration.

Do you think you could do that? As you can see, there is nothing to fear. This is why housewives, shop floor workers and professional people like bankers, solicitors, accountants, teachers and even ministers of religion succeed in this business. None of them would be seen dead trying to 'sell' in the traditional sense!

Chapter 4

Who Gets Involved?

The answer is—*anyone* and *everyone*!

The business, by its nature, genuinely does away with all the boundaries of discrimination which can help or hinder you in almost any other occupation, whether it be background or education, age, sex, race or colour, previous experience, wealth or lack of it. As a result, all kinds of people come into the industry, attracted by the opportunity to succeed by their own merits. You find this refreshing rainbow of variety from those just coming in, right up to those at the very top.

So it is easier to categorise people to whom network marketing might appeal more by what they want from the business than by their character, personality, social background or experience.

But, broadly speaking, the business might appeal to you if you are:

1. Happy with your present method of earning a living but looking for a supplementary income to help with holidays, a new car, the mortgage, school fees, a hobby, and so on;

2. Looking to take control of your life, perhaps by getting out of serious financial difficulties or work-related problems or seeking to realise your ambitions;

3. A high-flyer who wants to devote time and effort to your ambitions and who is looking for the greatest income return or the fastest career progression in return for your commitment;

...Or if you want to earn what you are worth rather than what someone chooses to pay you;

...Or if you prefer to be promoted on results rather than relying on corporate politics;

Just as in conventional business, there is a 'ladder' system of promotion, with clearly defined job titles and extra benefits as you go up. But, in network marketing, you promote yourself as your business grows, with no-one to hold you back;

4. Someone who might enjoy in network marketing a money-making social life and feeling of belonging;

5. Looking for a work environment where you can increase your self-confidence, learn to communicate better, enjoy greater appreciation for your efforts, learn to make the maximum use of your talents and generally get more out of life;

6. Attracted by one of the maxims of network marketing that 'You can only succeed by helping other people to succeed'. There can be few businesses where honesty, ethics and a genuine caring pay off in such a handsome way.

Many part-time network marketeers in the States contribute part or all of their income to favourite charitable causes. For people like nurses or social workers, it allows them to carry on their socially valuable jobs without sacrificing their lifestyle. Ministers of religion can use the business to fund their religious activities.

Why does the industry enjoy such a broad attraction?

Because, despite the fact that the personal benefits can be enormous and its income-potential is so high, the business is so simple that *anyone* can learn to do it.

Most of us, whoever we are and whatever our situation in life, get involved in network marketing because we are looking to improve our lives; we are seeking to solve what is called our **ATAC Equation**:

Abundant **T**ime, Abundant **C**ash

—**A**bundant **T**ime to do the things we want to do and **A**bundant **C**ash to do them with.

The ATAC Equation varies enormously from person to person: a hermit needs very little cash and has plenty of time. But a pleasure-seeking tycoon is going to have great difficulty in finding the time for both work and play and is going to need mountains of cash to indulge their lifestyle!

It follows from this that the more ambitious you are or the more you want for your family, the harder it will be to solve your ATAC Equation.

Here are some examples of people you see commonly in network marketing:

1. People looking for a part-time income or an additional profit centre; or perhaps who are unable (for maybe family or health reasons) to take on full-time employment;

2. Unqualified manual or shop-workers; people who are redundant or unemployed; or people who feel held back by discrimination on the grounds of race

or colour, age, sex, education, experience, social background or medical condition;

3. Entrepreneurs or self-employed people;

4. Professional people or people from a vocational or caring background;

5. Serious executives, managers or directors; chairpersons of corporations; or people aspiring to these dizzy heights.

The first exposure an accountant, banker or lawyer may have to network marketing is when a client asks them to check it out; countless times, this has resulted in the professional adviser coming into the business!

Chapter 5

What Does It Cost To Get Started?

At whatever level you want to get involved, *this is not a business which requires much capital.*

All *reputable* Independent Distributors (under the guidance of their network marketing company) will make it very clear to you that the *only* stock you ought to buy is that legitimately needed for samples or demonstration.

All other stock need be bought only *after* you have got an order for it. In this way, people with no money are not at a disadvantage and I know of no other potentially high-level business where the start-up cost really is within the reach of everyone.

To further protect you, under UK law the company is not allowed to accept more than £75 (including VAT) as a total of *all* payments (enrolment fee, stock, samples, sales aids and anything else they can think of) in your first seven days.

Also by law, the company cannot legally require you to attend any training for which you have to pay a fee (although I would strongly suggest that it is in your interests to take on board as much training as you can).

As a further safeguard, if you drop out *at any time* (even after several years in the business), you can legally require your company to buy back any unsold stock from you at 90% of what you paid for it (provided, of course, that it is undamaged and unused). There can be few businesses where the supplier can be forced to buy back the unsold stock for no reason.

All this makes network marketing one of the most risk-free businesses there is.

In many network marketing opportunities, you can (as in conventional business) qualify for a higher discount by buying a given quantity of stock; but it is not worth doing this unless you have money which is both available and surplus to your immediate needs. Although you are taking little risk (because of the 90% buy-back clause), there is no sense in depriving yourself in order to do this.

There may seem to be an advantage in buying in at a higher position but this is not so. After a few months, you cannot tell the Distributors who came in with the minimum stock possible from those who bought in at a higher level.

So resist all pressures to buy more than you feel comfortable with. In fact, if *any* pressure is put on you to buy more, your sponsor is not behaving in accordance with the ethics of the concept and, if the company is an ethical one, he or she is also acting outside its instructions.

Chapter 6

What's In It For You?

This depends on what you want from the business. People come in looking for a low-level commitment, a high-level commitment, or somewhere in-between. Generally speaking, someone looking for a low-level commitment is a part-timer and someone looking for a high-level commitment is aiming to become a full-timer as soon as possible.

Having said that, some Distributors earn as much from their part-time activity as from their full-time occupation.

Many people begin on a part-time basis, committing perhaps 10-15 hours per week, with the intention of building their network marketing business into a full-time career. In this case, *it is wise not to go full-time too soon*; wait until your income from network marketing develops to a level that allows you to do this without undue risk.

What attracts Part-timers?

1. Potentially high earnings

The potentially higher earnings (as compared with most part-time jobs) give you a genuine choice: do you work fewer hours to earn what you need, or do you work the same hours as you do now but earn, perhaps considerably, more?

2. The social life

This is a pleasant side-benefit. There is spontaneous and immediate acceptance of new people. Most enjoy the quick-but-lasting friendships which are forged among network marketeers, stemming partly from the fact that everyone actually enjoys what they are doing and partly because, perhaps for the first time in their lives, people feel free to do what they want to do and be who they want to be.

If this aspect might interest you, the best way to see it in action is to go to a meeting yourself.

3. Complete flexibility of hours

You work when *you* want to, not when someone else tells you to.

For instance, a mother can vary her work-patterns according to whether it is term-time or school holidays; a businessperson who is using their network marketing business as an additional profit-centre can cut back when their core business is busy and can use the extra time profitably when their core business is slack.

During the recession, many accountants, businesspeople and even solicitors, instead of sitting back and moaning about the state of the economy, used their periods of enforced idleness to good effect by spending more time on network marketing knowing that, if things improved in their 'day job', they could cut back on their network marketing business to compensate.

In fact, many enjoyed the experience so much that, even when business picked up, they still kept up their network marketing activities.

What attracts the full-timers or career network marketeers?

1. A high-level business with a minimal investment

We have already seen how little you need to get involved.

No matter how big your business gets, the only stock you will need could comfortably be kept under your stairs or in an out-of-the-way corner.

2. Minimal risk on stock purchase

As we have said before, you have a legal 90% buy-back clause in your contract.

3. Positive cashflow

Conventional businesses operate with negative cash-flow. This means that you get paid only *after* delivery. People who supply retailers take *on average* 60 days to get paid. In some industries, even that is fast payment!

Positive cashflow means that everything is cash-with-order. This is a protection against both overtrading and customer bankruptcy.

4. Exceptional earning potential

Unlike most conventional businesses, there is no theoretical limit to earnings. This is proved by the exceptional earnings which Independent Distributors can achieve. In many companies, the top distributors are earning substantial five-figure sums—per month! Most mature networks can show people who have retired wealthy two to five years from starting—often from a position of extreme financial hardship.

The USA industry claims that network marketing is now one of the main sources of new millionaires—

probably true since the collapse in property values. There is no reason for the same not to happen in the UK within the next few years.

5. Minimal overheads

No matter how big you get, you do not need:

- A warehouse
- Offices
- Staff
- Bank borrowings

6. Self-promotion based entirely on results

No waiting for 'dead-men's shoes', no relying on a superior's assessment of whether you are good enough.

People can, and do, get to the top position of a network marketing structure in one to three years, often achieving six or more promotions along the way. In normal business, a person does exceptionally well to get one promotion every two or three years, let alone reach the top in that time.

7. It is simple; anyone and everyone can do it

A business which allows everyone the same, and equal, access to the top has to be a good business. Apart from making a network marketeer feel good, this also means that you can show the business to *anyone* without having to worry about whether they have enough talent, intelligence of experience.

8. Security

Business or job security are now things of the past. Security comes from a potentially very high income which will allow you to build up capital. Security also comes from a saleable asset because you can sell your network on the open market; what is the market value of a business earning, say, £5,000 a month with no borrowings, liabilities, or the millstones of premises, staff or bad debts? Security comes from a business you can leave to your spouse or family if anything should happen to you.

What would happen to you now if you were made redundant, lost your job, or your company were to go bankrupt? Not a pretty thought, is it? But, if your network marketing company were to go bankrupt today or if its product were to stop selling, you could be up-and-running tomorrow in a new network. And, if you have looked after your Independent Distributors well enough, many of them would go with you.

That is the *real* security: being able to start up again tomorrow with a strong network of people who have moved with you.

9. Freedom

My previous business life, in common with so many people in conventional business, was constant worry— with personal guarantees up to the hilt, unco-operative local planners, unsupportive bank managers, and the sheer thrill of paying wages to those staff who did not appreciate the long hours we worked on their behalf.

Although I was my own boss and we were living a good life, I was never *free*! Many professionals and people in corporate business tell me that they feel the same way. Even though they may be on high incomes, the higher they go the longer the hours they have to work and the less free they become! In fact, *very few people feel free to live life the way* **they** *want to*. Do you? If so, you are one of the privileged minority.

If you would like an occupation that gives you greater freedom, network marketing may well offer the opportunity you are seeking.

Chapter 7

How Do You Assess A Company And Its Product?

It is so easy to get carried away by the excitement of a new proposition that even level-headed, experienced entrepreneurs—never mind those who are inexperienced in business—can, in the euphoria of the moment, overlook the most basic precautions.

If you decide to become a network marketeer you are, even on a part-time basis, going to be putting a lot of effort and commitment into your new business. So make sure the company and the product you choose are going to be worthy of your efforts!

It will pay you handsomely to remember two maxims:

*'Your business cannot **long-term** be more successful than the product.'*

'An Independent Distributor cannot be more successful than their network marketing company.'

One of the myths you will hear is that, in network marketing, you can only make the big money by getting in at the beginning.

This comment is true of companies with uncompetitive or poor-selling product, but you should steer clear of these anyway.

But it is *not* true of good companies with good product.

Why is it not true that you need to get in early?

1. If you join a mature network, you will have proof that you are getting a saleable product and a good company with proven staying power in the market place

2. People who get in early can rarely count on the level of training which a mature company should have developed. As we discussed, good training will make a great deal of difference to your success

3. All mature companies can show you network marketeers who are doing very well despite coming in late

4. Having a good, long line of Independent Distributors above you (these are called your 'Uplines'), means that you have all the more people you can call on to help you to build your business.

People several levels above you earn royalty or commission from your sales, which makes you *entitled* to ask for—and expect—help from them. I have personally experienced a start-up situation and I can tell you that the network marketeers who came in later had an easier time—and those who came in even later had an even easier time—because there were so many people on whom they could call for support.

With regard to new or start-up companies, network marketing is no different to any other form of commercial enterprise. Unproven companies in whatever market are significantly more likely to fail than established ones.

42

However, if you do get in with a rocket, you will, just as in conventional business, have greater opportunities to rise faster.

'New company, or old?' is really a case of 'horses for courses'. People who enjoy the challenge of a risk will go for the new, people who want security will go for the old. Ask yourself the question, 'If I were looking for a position in my *present* line of work, would I prefer a new company or a well-established one?' ... And apply the same rule when you are looking at network marketing companies.

If you are someone who likes to get in at the start, take no notice of those people who advocate that you should not consider any network marketing company unless it has been in the business for two years. On this basis, *no* new company would ever get off the ground—and, anyway, what about those people, myself included, who actually *like* to get in at the beginning?

Of course, a new company should be able to show you proof that it understands the concept of network marketing, which is so different to conventional business that if the company does not apply the system properly, it will fail. So take the time to have a look at the backgrounds of the directors—do they have relevant corporate or management experience? Also, many companies underestimate the resources needed to set up a sound network marketing operation—so ensure that the company is properly funded. Read also the Appendix (see page 53), which might help you to avoid some more obvious pitfalls.

Many network marketeers, if they are not from a commercial background, can misunderstand the importance of the product to the success of their businesses. Some networks can place so much emphasis on business-building by sponsoring, that the issue of how good the product is can get clouded.

Conventional companies use trained salespeople, sometimes heavy advertising and sales promotion to sell their products. So the quality of the product is often not as important as the amount of money poured into making it sell. As a result, you will find plenty of examples where the fastest-selling product is *not* the best one in that particular price-band; it is the one which has had the most money put behind it.

For instance, many supermarket shoppers buy expensive and heavily advertised branded products, even when the supermarket stocks 'own brand' products which offer the same quality at a lower price.

But network marketing uses an entirely different philosophy of retailing: people personally 'recommending' a product to friends, relations, neighbours and acquaintances, or to people introduced to them by friends, relations, neighbours or acquaintances.

If you are going to recommend a product to someone you know, or who has been introduced to you by someone you know, how will you need to feel about the product? Will you not need to feel that it is at least as good as anything else at that price on the market?

It is for this reason that good companies place such reliance on the product. As we saw, 95% of network marketeers neither are, nor will want to be, trained salespeople. If they do not feel good about the product then they will very soon stop recommending it.

To build a sound business, look for products which have a good Quality/Price Ratio. That is to say that they are at least as good as anything else at that price that is widely available in the market.

How can you tell whether a product or range has a good Quality/Price Ratio? That is easy—compare it with what else is available by going around the shops and keeping an eye out for mail-order advertisements. If possible, talk to a few people who know the market well.

But it is not enough that you feel comfortable with recommending the product—the people you recommend it to must also want to buy it! There are some excellent products on the market with only one fault: no-one wants to buy them! If this applies to your product, you shouldn't need me to tell you that you are not going to earn much money from it!

Therefore for products involving 'one-off' sales you should be looking for something which retails easily outside the network, which means is has a ready market to people who are not yet Independent Distributors. This can be somewhat less important with products or ranges which Independent Distributors are happy to keep using or 'consuming' themselves, so that everyone keeps earning from repeat orders. In these networks, regular users of the product often become Distributors in order to earn discounts on purchases for personal use and to do a little retailing to their friends. This can work well provided that there are also enough Independent Distributors working actively to bring in new business.

It is a fallacy that unique products necessarily network better. The new and unique product which the company is raving about may be a great idea, but do people actually want to *buy* it? The real criterion is whether it has a ready market, not whether it is unique.

It is also a fallacy that repeat products are necessarily better than 'one-off' sales. Network marketing is simply another way to retail a product. Just as there are traditional retailers earning a good living from selling 'one-off' products such as televisions, kitchen utensils and cars, so there are plenty of high-earning Independent Distributors handling 'one-off' products.

Much more important than whether it is a repeat product or a 'one-off' is: are you going to feel *proud* of it? If not, look for an alternative! Some people feel comfortable with one product, some with another. There is no 'right or wrong' here, only whether *you* feel happy with it.

To sum up, before you commit yourself to a network marketing company, you can do a fair bit of checking into whether:

- They have an experienced management team
- They are properly financed
- The product or range has a good Quality/Price Ratio
- Whether the products are selling outside the network, or whether they are sticking inside it
- Whether new distributors are given the quality training and support they need to make a winning start.

Chapter 8

What Can You Offer To The People You Know?

Becoming an Independent Distributor is not just about *you* getting excited by the opportunity in front of you. The important thing is, what can you offer to people you know? After all, if *they* do not get excited, there is not much point in you getting excited!

Network marketing is not just another business. It is a lifestyle opportunity—an opportunity for people, many of whom are having a not very good time one way or another, to change their lives to something better, or to get out of real problems. This means you have...

...The power to transform lives

Make no mistake about it—by developing a network marketing business you would have the power to transform the lives of everyone who chose to join you. The rest of this chapter will show what might excite people about this business and why Independent Distributors should feel proud of being part of this great industry. In this chapter, I summarise much of what has been said before, but from the point of view of people you know.

Meaningful and satisfying work

One of the most exciting things about network marketing is the satisfaction of the job itself. Doing work we dislike has a corrosive impact on our lives. Did you know that people who are unhappy with their jobs are three times more likely to get sick or die younger? And studies show that most people do hate their jobs. But Independent Distributors love what they are doing because they have the six things that people want most from their work—*freedom, meaning, companionship, the appreciation of others, the chance to earn what they want, and security.*

People dislike having their working lives controlled by others. They dislike taking orders, they dislike having to do things they have not chosen to do, and they dislike the fact that their promotions and pay awards are in the hands of others. Independent Distributors, in contrast, have control over their own working lives. They choose when they will work, how much they will work, where they will work and with whom they will work. And they enjoy self-promotion and 'award' themselves their own pay rises, based entirely on results. In short—they feel free to live the lives *they* want to live. *Do you find that attractive? Do you think that other people might find it attractive and want to join you?*

Again, most people feel that their work lacks meaning. The helping professions offer a deep sense of satisfaction and vocation. But, as any nurse or teacher will tell you, they feel underresourced, undervalued, underpaid and underappreciated. Through your business, you too will experience the deep satisfaction of helping people to solve major and minor problems in their lives and fulfil their true potential. You will see many of the people who join you blossom as they move from poverty and debt to financial independence, from failure to success, from self-doubt to self-confidence, from frustration to fulfilment. *Do you find that attractive? And do you think that other people might find it attractive?*

Many people lead isolated lives or work with people they dislike. In network marketing, there is spontaneous and immediate acceptance of new people. Because of the need to help each other to grow and develop in the business, Independent Distributors forge quick but lasting friendships and you will spend your time with a group of like-minded professional colleagues. *Do you find that attractive? Do you think other people might find it attractive?*

Bosses in traditional organisations are very bad at showing *heartfelt* appreciation of work well done and this trend is, if anything, getting worse. In almost every occupation, people are either leaving or are working with bad grace and minimum commitment when once they were loyal. It is like a great breath of fresh air to come into something like network marketing where, because you do not *have* to do anything, uplines and corporate teams really appreciate what you *do* choose to do. *Do you find that attractive? And do you think that other people might find it attractive?*

As well as the satisfactions of the work itself, network marketing has the potential to offer very high returns on every hour you invest in your business. Top earners achieve an amazing £200 to £300 or even more for every *hour* they work. Part-timers can earn more in 10 to 15 hours per week than they do from their full-time jobs. Part-time incomes of £10,000 to £15,000 per year are perfectly realistic with a good company. Full-time incomes potentially rise from this to a small number of top performers achieving substantial six figure sums—per month! *Do you find that attractive? Do you think other people might find it attractive?*

But money is meaningless unless you have the time to use it to do the things you value in life. It is important to understand that in the early stages you will be putting in long hours for little immediate return. There are no free lunches in this business—you have to *earn* the benefits! But, as your business matures and you develop a group of effective leaders, it will become increasingly possible to take time away *while the business continues to grow without you!* Is there any other industry where this can be achieved with no special skills and no previous experience? *Do you find that attractive? And do you think that others might find it attractive?*

Almost more than anything else, we live in a frightened society. In work, this means the fear of unemployment or bankruptcy, being thrown on the scrap heap in middle age, and the prospect of a very long enforced 'retirement' on a low pension. No matter how hard we work or how good we are at what we do, we no longer control our futures and that makes us, at best, feel very insecure. Network marketing gives security to those who work hard, learn the concept properly and apply it with vigour. *Do you find that attractive? And do you think that other people might find it attractive?*

So, in return for an initial investment of time and effort, network marketing will help you to solve your **ATAC Equation: A**bundant **T**ime to do the things you want to do and **A**bundant **C**ash to do them with.

And, what many people would find even more satisfying, through your business you can help many other people to solve their ATAC Equations.

Chapter 9

So, What Do You Do Next?

As I said in the Preface, although network marketing is a magnificent business concept, *this does not mean that it is right for everyone.*

I hope that now you can see this wonderful business in a new light. It may be that, even if you do not feel that the idea would benefit you at the moment, there are people you know for whom this could solve some small or serious problems in their lives. If so, why not lend them this little book or, if this was sent to you by a network marketeer, put them in touch with each other?

Of course, whether they are interested or not is their decision, but would you not be doing them a favour by giving them the option of looking?

Let me stress that, if you do decide to come into the business, the path ahead may not be an easy one— nothing worthwhile in life ever is! But do it right, do it with *commitment* and *determination*, *learn* from everyone around you and, above all, do it with *patience*, and you will, in time, join the ranks of those very many others for whom network marketing has led to a whole new panorama, a whole new enjoyment and a whole new quality of life.

If you want to investigate the possibilities more deeply then, if this book was lent to you by a network marketeer, they will arrange this for you.

It may be that their company runs meetings specially designed for people looking at the business for the first time. If so, you might find that going to one and seeing, not only what it is all about, but also the sort of people who get involved, would be helpful before you make a final decision.

If this book was not lent to you by a network marketeer, the Direct Selling Association (DSA), whose address is on page 10, will willingly help you to get the advice you need.

If you do decide to become involved, I hope you do so with the spirit of giving your opportunity a real chance. In every network, some Distributors achieve what they want while others do not, yet the opportunity is the same for both! So the key to success is not the product of the opportunity, it is *you*, the Distributor. Learn to respect and love what you do, and the business will love you. Commit to achieving what you want, commit to seeing it through, commit to learning and to applying it right, and it will repay you many times over in many ways.

But, whatever your choice, I wish you good health, enjoyment and fulfilment in everything you do.

Appendix

Corruptions Of The Concept

'It is no more sensible to judge this business by its abusers than it is to judge the medical profession or the building industry by their rogues.'

Network marketing is such a powerful concept that it has inevitably attracted its share of abusers. This Appendix should help you to avoid these unethical schemes.

What is Pyramid Selling?

What were generally called Pyramid Selling schemes had certain unacceptable characteristics which have now been outlawed.

The real problem was that Distributors got caught with large amounts of stock—and could do nothing about it. This was caused by the product increasing in price as it moved down the chain, until eventually some poor Distributor was caught trying to sell it on at more than it was worth.

How did the law stop this?

Very simply. As you saw earlier, if an Independent Distributor does want to drop out, the company has to pay them back 90% of what they paid for any unsold product, even if they have been in the business for several years.

This resulted in companies establishing set wholesale and retail selling prices—exactly as is done in traditional retailing. The benefit of this is that every Independent Distributor now has the opportunity to buy at the same basic prices.

In some schemes, the main income was from enrolment fees rather than from the movement of product. The law banned that as well, and now the only legal means of earning are from the proper sale and purchase of stock.

Avoid 'Matrix Plans' with no proper product

Matrix Plans have two hallmarks:

• The structure of your business is fixed by the company (e.g., a '5 x 12' matrix means that your matrix goes 5 wide and 12 deep)
• There is no 'self-promotion' possible (pages 30, 38)

The great majority of matrix plans offer a very inferior product. Some find ways around the law and pay on recruitment rather than the movement of product, so there is no incentive for anyone to sell anything. You should avoid any plan unless *all* your income comes from product sales.

Avoid 'Subscription-selling' schemes

In such schemes, you are paid on the sale of club subscriptions. You earn nothing from any products the members may buy. No such schemes have yet stood the test of time, because they are not based on the movement of stock.

Avoid Chain Letter systems and 'Money Games'

These either have no product at all, or use an inferior product as an excuse for passing money up the chain. Some of these money games are presented in a highly professional way, and can trap the unwary. Other favourite schemes are to offer either badly written books on 'How To Succeed' (or some other equally compelling-sounding title!), or subscriptions for worthless magazines on business opportunities.

And a final word of warning:

Avoid advertisements for Independent Distributors using an '0898' number.

Why? Because, not only does an '0898' call cost you more than a normal phone call, but the person who placed that advertisement actually makes a profit from you as well! If they have a genuine need for anonymity, they could just as easily have used a newspaper or Royal Mail box number, a secretarial agency or—best of all—a free '0800' number.

For safety, follow this simple rule

To summarise, you should be safe if you follow this simple rule:

'Avoid all schemes which do not generate your income exclusively from the sale of quality goods or services at a fair price'.

If you have any doubts at all about a business proposition, the DSA will be happy to help (see page 10).

International Addresses

Australia

Direct Selling Association Of Australia, Suite 1, 13 Business Park Drive, Notting Hill, VIC 3168
—Tel (61) 03 558 9352

Canada

Direct Sellers Association, 100 West Beaver Creek Road 3, Richmond Hill, Ontario L4B 1H4
—Tel (1) 905 886 8555

Hong Kong

Direct Selling Association Of Hong Kong Ltd., c/o Amway Asia Pacific Ltd., 26/F Citicorp Centre, 18 Whitfield Road, Causeway Bay
—Tel (852) 566 2239

Ireland

Direct Selling Association Of Ireland, Grand Canal House, Upper Grand Canal Street, Dublin 4
—Tel (353) 01 667 1146

Netherlands

Vereniging Direkte Verkoop, Postbus 90154, NL - 5000 LG Tilburg
—Tel (31) 13 944300

New Zealand

Direct Selling Association Of New Zealand, P.O. Box 28245, Remuera, Auckland 5
—Tel (64) 09 520 2044

Singapore

Direct Selling Association of Singapore, Newton P.O. Box 127, Singapore 9122
—Tel (65) 747 6006

South Africa

Direct Selling Association, c/o Johannesburg Chamber Of Commerce & Industry, Private Bag 34, Auckland Park 2006
—Tel (27) 011 726 5300

Just what is...
Network Marketing?

Your down-to-earth introduction to the low risk business opportunity that has brought prosperity, fulfilment and personal freedom to thousands around the world

David Barber
F.Inst.S.M.M. F.Inst.D.

INSIGHT Network Marketing Library

Group leader?
Book distributor?

We can supply this book at quantity discounts.

For further details, ring the Insight orderline on:

01989-566600

"I'd Like To Sign Up, But...
How Do I Get My Business Off To A Winning Start?"

New! *For the first time, an inspiring British self-study programme reveals ALL the inside knowledge you need to succeed in network marketing.*

Starting your new network marketing business is exciting but it can also be a little daunting. If you are like most new distributors, you will be thinking:

- Can I *really* succeed and earn the money they say I can?
- I have never done anything like this before—I don't know if I would be any good at selling.
- How can I show the people I recruit how to succeed in this business? I hardly know where to begin myself!

No matter how little confidence or experience you may have, David Barber's **S.T.A.R. Leadership Programme** will give you ALL the help you need to build your business step by step, from the very first phone-call to the most advanced leadership techniques. If you are committed to creating a professional, ethical and *enjoyable* business and helping your people to do the same, then you will find no better guide!

The S.T.A.R. Programme is founded on the well-proven truths of network marketing and self-development. But David Barber is a great teacher and communicator, and has developed exciting new tools which make the business easier to learn and easier to teach to others. Now you, and everyone you bring into the business, can achieve your goals in network marketing. All you need are determination, a willingness to learn, and some help from David Barber's new books:

- *Get Off To A Winning Start In Network Marketing (Feb '96)*
- *Breakthrough Sponsoring & Retailing (Feb '96)*
- *How To Lead A Winning Group (April '96)*
- *Network Marketeers—Supercharge Yourself! (April '96).*

Here is the *new* solution
to all your training needs!

Outstanding new materials

At last! A full range of quality **British** training and sponsoring materials. to help you:

• Inspire your contacts about network marketing

• Give the best possible start to your new distributors

• Develop high-level leadership skills

• Improve motivation and goal-setting.

Don't miss out on the biggest training development in years. Just ring and ask for details of our full range of exciting professional materials.

Mail-Order Book, Video and Tape Service

Looking for the very best in training and motivational materials from around the world? If you have any difficulty in purchasing what you need through your network, the Insight mail order service will be delighted to help!

Volume Supplies

If you are a book distributor or group leader, contact us for details of our discount book service. We can supply all titles in the Insight Network Marketing Library, together with a selected range of the very best training and motivational tools and resources. And if you are thinking of setting up a new book service within your company, we can offer you *free* training and advice.

Training Consultancy

Why not get David Barber working for *you* and your leaders? His new Leadership Development Seminar is already earning rave evaluations from some of the most experienced network marketeers in the UK. Learn the new training techniques that really make a difference and cascade them down your group. Cut drop-out rates and watch your business take off!

This service really is something special—it's going to take the industry by storm. And it's much more affordable than you might think. For the best investment you can make in your business, contact us today for information!

Contact us NOW for full information about these exciting new services and we will send you:

- **A FREE catalogue and newsletter**
- **A valuable bonus report.**

Just ring our order-line on:

01989-566600

for fast and friendly service.

If you prefer, you can fax *01898-565596...*

...or write to:

Insight Publishing
Serendipity House
Greytree Road
Ross-on-Wye
Herefordshire
HR9 7DQ

using the order form overleaf $\rightarrow$

Yes!

Please send me regular news about new publications and training services from Insight Publishing.

Please send me my FREE catalogue and newsletter, plus bonus report.

Name _____

_____

Address _____

_____

_____

Postcode _____

Telephone _____

Your Network Marketing Company

_____

Please mail to:

Insight Publishing
Serendipity House
Greytree Road
Ross-on-Wye
Herefordshire HR9 7DQ

db/pros